BRIGHT RAFT

IN THE

AFTERWEATHER

VOLUME 82

Sun Tracks
An American Indian Literary Series

SERIES EDITOR

Ofelia Zepeda

EDITORIAL COMMITTEE

Larry Evers

Joy Harjo

Geary Hobson

N. Scott Momaday

Irvin Morris

Simon J. Ortiz

Craig Santos Perez

Kate Shanley

Leslie Marmon Silko

Luci Tapahonso

BRIGHT RAFT IN THE

AFTERWEATHER

POEMS

JENNIFER ELISE FOERSTER

**THE UNIVERSITY OF
ARIZONA PRESS**

TUCSON

The University of Arizona Press
www.uapress.arizona.edu

ISBN-13: 978-0-8165-3733-4 (paper)

Cover design by Leigh McDonald
Cover art adapted from *Extinction #2* by H Matthew Howarth

Publication of this book is made possible in part by the proceeds of a permanent endowment created with the assistance of a Challenge Grant from the National Endowment for the Humanities, a federal agency.

Library of Congress Cataloging-in-Publication Data
Names: Foerster, Jennifer Elise, author.
Title: Bright raft in the afterweather : poems / Jennifer Elise Foerster.
Other titles: Sun tracks ; v. 82.
Description: Tucson : The University of Arizona Press, 2018. | Series: Sun tracks : an American Indian literary series ; volume 82
Identifiers: LCCN 2017042838 | ISBN 9780816537334 (pbk. : alk. paper)
Subjects: | LCGFT: Poetry.
Classification: LCC PS3606.O39 B75 2018 | DDC 811/.6—dc23 LC record available at https://lccn.loc.gov/2017042838

Printed in the United States of America
♾ This paper meets the requirements of ANSI/NISO Z39.48-1992 (Permanence of Paper).

To Magdalena, almost visible

CONTENTS

IV. THE OUTER BANK

ACKNOWLEDGMENTS

To my teachers, friends, and family: thank you for your generosity, wisdom, and encouragement, without which I could not have written this book. Thanks to those who read and offered suggestions for some of these poems, especially: Eleni Sikelianos, Bin Ramke, Graham Foust, Carolina Ebeid, Taryn Schwilling, Brian Foley, David Walter, dg nanouk okpik, Joy Harjo, Cedar Sigo, Sonja Kravanja, and Rosemary McCombs Maxey. So much of this work was made possible by the time, space, and provisions of the Lannan Foundation Writing Residency Fellowship, the Caldera Artists in Residence Program, the University of Denver, and the National Endowment for the Arts. I am grateful to my faculty and peers at the University of Denver's Department of English, who have been immensely inspiring and supportive.

The poems in this collection have been published (sometimes under a different title) in the following journals:

The Brooklyn Rail. "Land Art."
Bronze Chimes: Poems for Alfred Starr Hamilton. "River."
Colorado Review. "Inheritance," "Wallpaper."
Drunken Boat. "Lost Coast."
Eleven Eleven. "The Painter."
Ghost Town. "Apricots."
The Kenyon Review (KROnline). "Paradise," "Pilot."
LitHub. "Undertow," "Sail."
Mud City Journal. "Catch."
NECK. "Descent."
OAR. "The Last Kingdom," "The Floating World."
Orion. "Winter Watch."
Past Simple. "Hoktvlwv's Crow," "Touring the Earth Gallery."
POETRY. "Canyon."
PoetryNow! "The Other Side."
The Rumpus. "Afterweather."
TriQuarterly. "Refrain."
Visible Binary. Selections from "Of" (section title pages).
World Literature Today. "Resurrection."
Yellow Medicine Review. "Old Woman and the Sea."

BRIGHT RAFT

IN THE

AFTERWEATHER

BEFORE THE HURRICANE

Acropolis of / clouds
  Wreckage of / *a distant slope*
Act of / violence
  Wreath of / *mussels*
Allegory of / shore
  Wings of a / *whales*
Angels of / light
  Window of / *ships*
Angle of / trees
  Window of / *marsh birds*
Arrangement of / seashells
  Whip of / *waves*
Arrows of / seeds
  Village of / *oars*
Back of a / wolf
  Veil of / *bait*
Base of a / fjord
  Vanishing of / *the gulls*
Beating of / birds
  Upthrusts of / *trolling boats*
Beats of / bells
  Type of / *crab traps*
Bed of / gauze
  Two of / *the sea*
Beds of / ice
  Train of / *scales*
Bird-palace of the / day
  Trail of / *stars*
Blades of / lovegrass
  Tracks of / *the Milky Way*
Blue of a / bluestem
  Trace of / *land*
Bones of / hands
  Tongues of your / horizon
Bottom of / January
  Tinkling of / *the farmhouse*
Bottom of the / world
  Tiers of / *the dying sun*
Boundary of the / field
  Thunderclouds of / *town*
Boundary of my / feet
  Thunder of / *antelope*
Bowl of / apricots
  Thrumming of / *rain*
Bowls of / milk
  Throats of / *leftover snow*
Branches of / hair
  Throat of / god
Breast of / granite
  Terrain of / snow
Bucket of / fish
  Tent of / *your shadow*
Buckets of / clay
  Teeth of / clouds
Burrs of / chinkapin
  Tail of / *birds*
Buttons of his / shirt
  Symmetry of / *snow*
Buzz of / words
  Swim of / *the mountain*
Cacophony of / gulls
  Surface of / clouds
Calligraphy of / thunder
  Stumps of / gods
Canyon of / snow
  Strokes of / *your dive*
Cascades of / willows
  Stroke of / air
Casements of / seeds
  Stretch of / *breath*
Chimera of a / horse
  Streets of / *granite*
Clatter of / 2:00 AM
  Streets of / grass
Clouds of / antelope
  Streams of / *black*
Clutches of / mussels
  Streaming of / *grass*
Coils of / stars
  Stream of / *lovegrass*
Coliseums of / light
  Straw of / *iris*
Collapse of / island states

Straw of the / Rhizomes of / afternoon the / continent
Rush of / Blue of / an / convent
Constancy of / Field of / an / cottonmouths
Stream of / Proportion of calcified / an / crab traps
Crush of / Points of / algae the / cypress
Clouds of / Field of / antelope the / day
Bowl of / Static of / apricots travelling / dead
Bucket of / Tent left of / ash / dead
Ribbons of / Highway departing of / bait / digression
Phantom of / Metals windy of / barges / dining car
Throat of / Specters of / back the / farmhouse
Shepherds of the / Tree of / basilica bath the / Dodo bird
Beats of / Coliseums of / belle / dusk
Shadows of / Towns of / berry / dust
Coliseums of / birds / birds my / ear
Clothing of / Pails smoke of / birds / egg
Piths of / Beats of / black / eye
Field of / Sheet of / black / face
Shades of / Boundary of / bluestem my / familiar
Shore of / Edge town of / bluestem the / fish
Mastery of / Streets of / body heaped / forty
Fragment of / Corner of / body the frozen / field
Lips of an empty / Instagrams of / bottle / field
Tent of / / birds the / fire
Thunder of / Outer reaches of / a travelling / dive
Mouths of / Creases of / charcoal her / fjord
Burrs of / Gutters of / chimneys / flowers
Landscape of / Mollusk drained of / chinkapin / fly
Skeleton of / Raft of a / city the / feet
Hands of / Bowls of / glacial city / fossils
Acropolis of / Names of / clouds / freight trains
Reflections of / Naming of / all my / Gastouri
Slab of / Arrangement of / clouds / gauze
Edge of / Shawl the of / concrete / giant
Edge of / Beating the of / continent / giants
Stairs of / Name the of / continent the / glass
Streams of / Skin of / flightless / god
Stacks of / Edge of / convent the / god
  / / cottonmouths the
  / / crab traps

OLD WOMAN AND THE SEA

A star, the sun, was born in the dark.
Salt leached from rocks.
The ocean rusted.

Hoktvlwv and I are talking
at the shore beside the tin carcasses.

I dressed you in gas clouds,
meteorites and dust,
coral-encrusted cables pulled from the sea.

The continent drapes its burnt cape behind us.

Hoktvlwv hums.
A ship's light passes.

Lava, ash
and song began us.

The foam drags back,
unclenches its hand.

Stiffened shells—
sea's ears—grip at the banks,
sand dollars clink at our feet.

What the sea returns
is enough, she writes, the words
over dunes shift, hissing.

Hoktvlwv stacks bright
coins in her cart,
clears a briar path.

Cliffs, lit with embers,
flicker out their blooms.

Her tracks are jagged and deep.

* *Hoktvlwv* — /hoktálwa/ n. old woman, elderly woman (Mvskoke)

THE FLOATING WORLD

18th Street at twilight
    lime trees
tikis in porticoes

A painter is painting
    Hunters in the Snow
beneath salt wind's rum shades
    smog-browned magnolias
                pale blue blooms of forage

    Listing south to the factories
with a silk corsage
    dusty crinoline callas
hinged to the stem with rusted pins

    I am not far from home, walls
humming with language—
    violent stalks
wild in the weave

and yet all my words
    listeners in concrete
graphite sketches
                suspended in air

    ice mass, methane, oxide soot

stones I plow
from my balcony box, potted lemons
skunks kick down

I look up at the woodcut moonlight

surfacing as if from lithograph ink
a nude girl leaning on a tree stump

flickering marquee

fuchsia's anxious splash

The flower shop's gate locks and I text you
a sonograph—mockingbirds
belting from streetlamps

our awkward failures
this city and its cloying fog

We will drown beneath the blue
curve of history anyway

and it won't matter, the petals
you pinned to my dress—

my consolation
this city's fragrant death

WINTER IN CORFU

I would have kept us as we were
above the village of Gastouri
in winter, pensiones closed,
vineyards ripe with kumquats, fennel,
stray cats crouching under rain pipes,
olive nets damped down with mud.

Even though it was not our island.
Not our goats to unchain from the hills'
Phaeacian ruins' overgrown rockrose,
each branch scraping starfish from the sea,
each beach a frieze of Odysseus's shipwreck.

I would have kept us as we were,
the road to Perithia brocaded shut with ferns,
stone fields fevered with poppies
and Mount Pantokrator sloped with crocuses
where we walked to that high monastery,
gold-headed thistles igniting the apse.

Even though it was not our god,
not our haunted basilica halls
of fog's high tides, Ionian clouds like
goat horns crowning icon kiosks
or priests swinging rust-gold lanterns
darkening storefronts of lingerie
that line the sun-bleached promenades
of gold-foiled chocolates, baklava bakeries,
dim bulbs half-lighting skinned lambs on hooks—

even at that bottom of January,
the sirocco blowing through Judas trees,
Santas noosed from loose shutter hinges,
a freezing rain hoofing over roofs,
and the two of us, embers in an emptying tavern
with an out-of-tune bouzouki band,
spinach pie and gritty wine,
I would have kept us as we were,
knowing that the spring would bring
its umber clouds above the sea,
a casino recolonized by black moss
and tulips, and Calypso's spellbound
mirage of an island, shingled with egrets,
would fade in the trade winds
as the fishing boats flash off
their last-catch starboard lights
and the Virgin of Kassiopi,
saint of sailors, throws
her crossbones overboard,
blows our votive out.

SAIL

A butterfly supernova
    spreads its silken winds.

    Sea's heavy snowflakes
        feather from shore.

The reef blinks, electric eels
           slip beneath the rock's lip.

    o

Our boat is a drowning cloud.
We follow the tide's
wet-black eyes.
Canting the shoals—
glass worms, shells.
I tell you the moon
has floated beneath us.
    A wave sweeps in,
stirs the clams. Crabs in their caverns
fan their claws as you and I,
scavengers for stars,
tin scraps stuck in mud flats,
float past the seawall's clutches
of mussels, encircled by harbor seals
swimming under dusk.

    o

On a drowning boat we drifted
south, counting moons,

humps of whales,
white pearls thrown by waves.

Sea, you said
you were never mine.

But I am always yours.

The stars are your wreckage—

ships I have lost.

○

Spiny urchins
ink,
swell.

Flesh—
ripped off the coral animal.

My chest,
a rusted music box,
chimes of dying reefs.

Day after day I open it.

Salty coffin,
seahorse wreathed,

how will I call you—

cloud scar?

Salve of grass

         o

Beyond the snow's
    white-capped shores—

        sea-ears heaped on the valley's floor.

Once mangrove coasts
    now ship-break yards.

Hubcap, shark finch, buzz of—words
are never enough, they do not make fire

nor rain for burning tankers,
beached infernal whales.

        o

Casting ribbons of entrails
to a squawking sequence of gulls
above the outrigger poles of trolling boats'
darkened windows, stacks of crab traps—
time is a raft of clouds when clean
swept are the tire-stapled railings of the sea
and dreamless, the fishermen
slapping on their rubbers,
sloshing buckets of bloody scales
in the star's cold machinery.

        o

The echo of your oars
outside my window

still wakes me.

A flock of marsh birds
beats through fog.

When I open my mouth, my breath
steams the glass.

There is nothing to say
or trace on the sea.

Pulpit overgrown with grass.

o

Our boat is neither sky
nor sea.

We are windowed in a narrow bunk
watching the mast compass stars,
night wind rattle the sails.

Maybe we should head south
I tell you, the moon, a lantern fish
drifts over glass. I trace
the swim of Andromeda,
skim the coast of your back.

A breeze takes shape
across black-lit waters—
        sails luff
                windward, my hands.

THE LAST KINGDOM

Three days before the hurricane
a woman in white is hauling milk.

The beach wails.
She is swinging her pail.

I am sleeping in a tent of car parts, quilts
when the woman passes through the heavy felt door.

If your dream were to wash over the village, she says.
We listen—seagulls resisting the shore.

Hermit crabs scuttle under tin.
The children hitch their sails in.

Later that night from the compound walls
I see her hitchhiking the stars' tar road—

black dress, black boots, black bonnet,
a moon-faced baby in a basket.

         o

    Thus, alone, I have conceived.

A tent dweller moved to the earth's edge,
I bathe in acidic waves.

Everyone in the village
watches at the cliff the tidal wave
breach, roll across the sky.

They are feasting on cold
fried chicken, champagne—
  I have no dancing dress for the picnic.

The king dozes in his gravelly castle.
The band plays its tired refrain.

Men, drunk on loosened wind
raise their cups to mechanical dolphins
tearing through the sheet-metal sea.

In the shadow of petrels'
snowy specters, drifting monuments
crash and calve.

But I, as water under wind docs,
I tear my hair,
scalp the sand—

the sun, eclipsed by dark contractions
turns its disc to night—

fish like bright coins
flip from my hand.

    o

  Waking, I find I am alone in the kingdom.

The moon lays upon me
its phosphorescent veil.

The floating world—luciferous:
bleached coral coliseum,

a mermaid's molten gown—

she turns her widening wheels,
spills her pail of glacial milk.

I could almost swim forever
to her beat of frozen bells.

But a sheet of water
doesn't travel with the wave.

And the morning like a tender body
slides out of silt:

I press against its damp
rough surface, an ear.

CANYON

Brush over star's dust,
upthrust shale,
erosion-stripped script of ledges—

sloughing scales off
our hands' finned imprints,
slow-aging metamorphic skins
    quartz
           schist
                gypsum—
marine bones bedded in the drainage.

The basin overflows with wind.
Horizon—phantom barges,
a shore once lush with cane.
Moon—a relic in the azure sky,
gray face cut from the mountain's spine.

A line of dust divides us—*narwhale*
and ghost—ancient stream
whose sound remains
    floodland
           arroyo
   yucca
           saguaro

I dive with pipevine swallowtails
down winding stairs, crenulated lava—
scrolls, fossilized in radiant strata, read
    prickly pear

silver cholla
            spicules of sponge

Here in this rain-shadow's stark
flanked gully, two blue-bellied lizards
streak across sand—vanish
inside a conch shell. *Arrived*
at the bottom of the world, I write.

Buried in the canyon's
spiraled larynx—
        a raft for the coming storm.

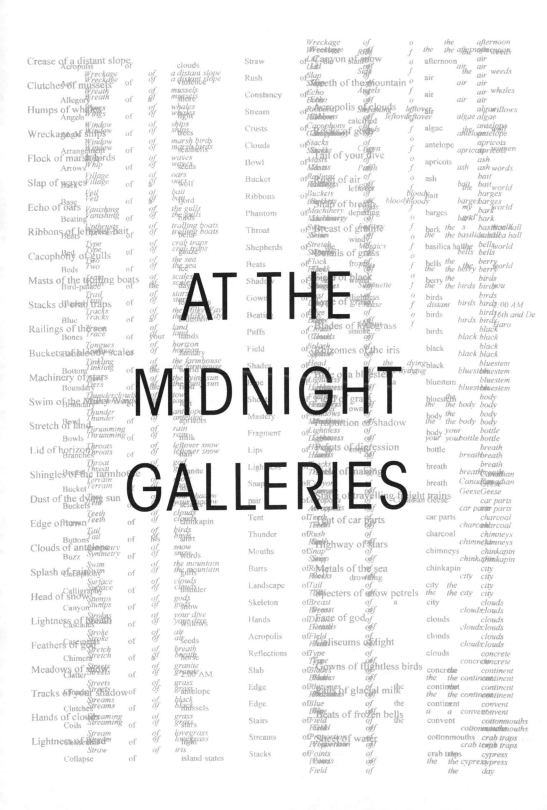

BLOOD MOON TRIPTYCH

PALIMPSEST

> We watched the eclipse
> under burnt-out street lamps
> until we darkened into the same
>
> imprint: bone, tree,
> every other breath
> one of ocean.
>
> Moon,
> earth fragment,
> remember us.

ECLIPSE

> Time is so demanding
> wearing out all the linens—
>
> the parchment, tablets,
> my evening melody.
>
> As if the margins
> were attempting to cross
> the poem, corpse
>
> of the corpus,
> moon's imprinted veil.

VEIL

Stumble past cypress
to the cliff's edge—

below you the town's lights
blink—extinguished.

Orion, the giant
walks blind over water.

What you see in the waves
are not stars: look up!

Bright net cast across
still-frosted pines—

leafy sea dragons,
ballerina eels.

You drift, a planet
forgotten in the infinite

body—dashed
on a soundless stone.

The clot in the sky
is not the moon

but blood—the body
you turned against.

TOURING THE EARTH GALLERY

Chicks—dead in a once teeming reef
and a mother bird
scouring ghostly coral.

We dozed, broke our machines.

Extreme heat, intensifying rain
will bring the island states' collapse,
a fast decline of sea grass.

Our time period is one of
glacial isostatic adjustment.

In the third chamber, dust
daily rearranged into pastoral scenes:

beach strewn with radioactive crustaceans—

"The Woman at Repose
with the Sea Behind Her."

Note that it is not the woman's
figure that is kinetic
but the structures above her:

fugitive lightning,
skeleton of a Dodo bird.

There, where a poet scrapes
her tail across tundra—

see the sand blowing over
her last regret.

She dips her quill into a pigment jar,
scrawls her forecast across the clouds:

    neon-blue antlers,
        cellular squid.

Smacked into glass
that resembled the sky—a sparrow
sleeps on its side in the dirt,

    yellow-feathered, wind-stuffed.

PILOT

Circling, your wooden wings
claw at wind—

wind in a canyon
once a sea
where floods once reached
the tails of birds
clinging to clouds by their beaks.

You are scaling the mountain's
time-cut teeth, chert face
packed with black trees, ice,

to weave a rope of sun—
gazing to heaven,
eyelids waxed shut.

I track your shadow
over gesso snow,

cross the widening plains beneath
shifting hands of fog,

kick the rocks of gods—
their tridents and stumps,
stony mouths.

Aerial somersault,
downdraft of sound—

I see you falling.
The ploughman keeps ploughing.

There was no angler to pull you out.
And this time you weren't falling from the sky.

No shepherds to witness the tail of your dive,
no purposeful ship masts passing by.

Your legs were not corkscrewing from the water.

No rush of air in your falling.
No final gasp, the snap—
no breath.

I bank the rocky ramparts,
pitch against the rain.

A shadow wings over granite.
Conifers drop their sapphire stones.

I stow one under feathers, tuck
the other under tongue—

I can almost see forever
you had said
three miles above the earth.

UNDERTOW

You were using a horsehair brush,
strokes for sunrise

over tundra, thunder's
black calligraphy.

As if the wind were slow milk.

White oil on cloth—
I'd been walking along a sculpted beach.

Is it not enough
you painted a portrait of him

led him after class
into your beach house

wrung a rope
around his neck

crowned him
a Trojan of the undersea?

THE PAINTER

Staining the canvas
titanium white
is an act of violence.

A woman's
fragment of body
surfaces like a fish.

The various shades of black
to be pulled from compressed charcoal
can be useful for the study
of snow, or a woman, naked
in a white window
dressing her shadow.

Or is it an ink sketch of a woman
washing her hair
upside down in a bathtub?

Your memory of her shifts
with a second coat.

The indeterminacy of mauve
is a multivalence,
red sun in a blue sky,
an allegory of a western shore
where she stands at the still pool
clutching a rose,
her hand on the stem
almost visible.

You are painting the bones
of your hands, not hers.

Or is it a painting of a girl
pulling up roots
at the base of a Norwegian fjord
under thunder—charcoal, linseed oil—
with a freight ship in the distance.

Lay a fresh ground on the painting
and start over: lavender
instead of roses. Ghost
instead of limb.

You relearn the procedure. This one
is about layering.
It is based on a Polaroid:
tourists at the cliff,
a woman falling from the sky.

You coat her with amber shellac.
Layering the light over her,
you want to light the brutality
but the light itself
obscures brutality.

With ochre strokes you tug her to bay,
paste her withered wings with wax
and there she sleeps in a gauze bed.

It is a piece about the recollection of skin
and that is all.

A painting of five empty chairs.
Lilacs in the window frame
between two mirrors. There is Lilith
in a kitchen frock
hemmed with roses.
There is Grace, dragging
their shadow across linoleum.

The red is embroidery, yellow—
canvas. Black the basic idea.
Coffee, tea, or ink—rejected materials
and you are meant to respond to the stain.

You paint her border with a smoke's thread.
Wipe the cloth. Draw an arc.
Decoupaged, the painting is dead.
Her gods have destroyed it.

It was a rebellion.
A mastery of her own body.

You have tried sandbags.
Suspension cords.
Every kind of seeing.

You have silk screened
her image on the wall,
left the screen on the floor
as a residue of the process.

You have strung her pink heart
to the apple branch,
eaten her horsehair comb.

In your abandoned studio
a derailed chair.
A photograph of two women
among burning trees.

The pages dust
your window like snow.
Little black-noted you,
rearranging yourself on the wall.

There are many ways
of rearranging dust—
these are the dark strokes.

INHERITANCE

You do not see her immediately

               red-ochered Beothuk

    White syllable

                     sailing into the spheres

Her beach camp remains

               dead fire, snare

She travels through mist

                   the way a poem travels

by fuel, high winds

               skiff of fox fur

  auk's eggs

             oily words

dropped into the sea

             You are witness but do not see

the wave form's irregular patterning

                entrails, seal skin

Her skull among the Skraelings' skulls

             sailing north to Scotland

LAND ART

Think about a word: *grass*—

about an individual grass
then about a hundred species of grass.

At first you look and see a large field.

Look closer and you will see
the grasses in the field.

We are standing, boxed by a hot window,
our back to the fields.

Lift the grasses from a box
and lay them out across the field.

A man picks up
a golden stalk—

claw-like
slender auricles
clasped at the blade.

Don't worry about your grasses
falling apart—grasses
grow to disintegrate!

When a grass falls apart
you have a chance to notice
each individual floret—

what separates one grass
from another.

On the paspalums grass:
　　　sessile spikelets.

　　　　　　On the Panicums grass:
　　　　　　　　broad basal notes.

Scattered along the axis
we form a rosette—

　we are bunched, decumbent culms,
　　　the involute blades of love grass.

　　　　See how the branches effloresce?

　　Count the glumes.
　　　They will put out seeds.
　　They will begin to reveal themselves—

　　　　　　Buffalo grass

　　　　　　Witchgrass

　　　　　　Black bent

　　　　　　Barley

The people in the church begin to talk
like leaves with ciliate ligules—

　　If you split the rhizomes

of the iris in summer.

I've never seen the blue
of a blue stem, says another.

We are tiny radiating windmills
at a dinner party of grass.

Dissect the seed head.

Peel the sheath.

Oh flutists of space,

windblown graminoid—

walk into the greenly singular, singing

the long sight line,

monochrome field.

If you don't understand

what the symphony is saying,

how the wind plays harps with the grass—

note its scale change:
to the north

one pronghorn

freezes in the meadow—

fine fescue

monocotyledon.

Note the digression—field

to frame. How the setting

down of art

is as important as its making.

Turn from the grass to the fields
out the window.

You will look for patterns

and see none.

You will look for openings—

they will close to you.

The light in each grass fast fading—

we lie down in this dark.

AFTER I BURY THE NIGHTINGALE

Pails of glacial milk of the sea
Beats of frozen bells of an island
Sheet of water of my ear
Boundary of my feet of god's face
Edge of the continent of men
Streets of heaped glass of an empty bottle
Corner of 16th and De Haro
Instagrams of high wires
Perfume of night-blooming cereus
Lights of the dead
Outer reaches of a fracturing hand
Creases of her palms
Bowls of milk
Names of the missing
Gutters of Telegraph Hill
Raft of reeds
Mollusk of my ear
Shawl of flowers
Arrangement of seashells
Naming of you
Beating of birds
Skin of the sea
Name of all things
Edge of the continent
Landscape of a drowning city
Skeleton of a city
Flutes of your music
Gray of the visible world
Raft of seaweed
Creases of my palms
Thrumming of pigeons
Drum of rapturous waves
Village of Gastouri
Frieze of Odysseus's shipwreck
Shepherds of the windy basilica halls
Storefronts of lingerie

Bottom of January
The two of us
Mirage of an island
Angle of trees
Throat of bark
Branches of hair
House of hours
Stirrups of a wild horse
Necklace of thorns
Clatter of 2 am
Boundary of the field
Map of the world
Wreath of weeds
Haze of flies
Face of night
Seat of a cross-town train
Netting of blue veins
Scent of her father skull
Feather of this morning's nightingale
Host of moths
Fin of the first star
Mouth of the river
Sound of ships
Mouths of chimneys
Glade of shade pine
Coils of stars
Fractals of falling hours
Sighs of porpoises
Wings of swimming snails
Rain of the dead
Cracks of the gas-lit shore
Train of shark fins
Terrain of the in-between
Eyes of fish
Creek of the back forty
Straw of the slant afternoon

REFRAIN

There is a woman who whistles
from the arroyo—*oh hollow bone*
you have a body you cannot carry alone.

What I carry beneath an ocean
same color as the sky
is not my own

though I am always yours,
collecting fractals of falling hours,
coral scales for your necklace.

Nightly I fall from my skin
to the surface—glass worms
drift in the trade winds,
sighs of porpoises billow the dunes.

Beneath the swimming Sargassum blooms,
snails' sapphire wings,
I depend on the rain of the dead for food—
my umbrella, flared, is a fossil.

Oh abyssal fish with telescope eyes,
fish with luminous torches,
where are the whirling Spanish dancers?
Where are my drowned teeth, ear bone, jaw?

A crab marches its marbled shell
across the ocean floor—
         as if the body was ensnared
         by its own memory.

Body, I drag you like a shipwreck,
pluck the pelican-trampled weeds
from the cracks of the gas-lit shore
to fasten into your hair nest—

and some days can only manage
to sit on the deck with a cigarette
watching the tin clouds rust in the rain,
my fish-shaped bath soaps
bleed into gutters
no longer knowing blue
from blue, flesh from light,
sea from sky. I cannot echo

your absence without dissolving you,
cannot retrieve you from rock
or from sound, nor can I return you.

A freight train carrying last night's dreams
steams across the in-between
where I wait at the depot catching dust,
holding a suitcase and your clammy hand—
    where the eyes of fish
    are not windows

but moons the earth
has forgotten. Like a bone
afloat on a darkening sea
the arroyo's fluted
surface whistles—
    Body, have you forgotten me
    so soon?

THE OTHER SIDE

My crown.
My room.
Surrounding snow.

These are not my
hands, my winter shoes
carried off by uncertain music.

There was a meadow
behind my house
and if I should see myself there
she would tell me
there was never a meadow

and then walk through me
as if through a cloud
and carry on in her own
solitary direction.

Crows still caw
in her palace garden—
tram rails, rain,
stammering moon.

Once lilacs bloomed
their huge white knuckles
breaking the winter of my room—

it was a dream—French windows
on a Viennese street.

Every street I cross
angling alongside
smoggy postwar artifices

branches scratch
against my sleep.

How my body was a branch
in my sleep.

And when I woke
years later
I peered down upon it
leafless and stiff.

No roosts left, no caw.
No birds blooming
in the dream's green crooks.

Afternoons alone
are labyrinthine.
I wander the city, searching
for what? Friends,
we knew where to find each other,
tapping the window of the winter room.

We were thinner then,
younger than the chestnut trees.

Everything has its seed
much later
and on the other side of time.

RESURRECTION

Summers we lie out on the hot porch
    palms splayed—

raising flames from ragweed,
    hoofed dancers of the hayfield,
        tornado's sharp-toed steeds.

In the rusted truck behind the barn
a tufted titmouse sings

    balled up like a stone,

        stick claws stiff as thorns.

When the nest of starlings
built in the eaves

    drops a hatchling,

      we steal its pink
      body to the roof,

        lay it out beneath the lightning.

Our mouths creak open
    to honeyed light—

      Tie-Snake, stag-horned,
        binds our feet.

NIGHTINGALE

I've heard the nightingale tapping at the window,
seen her singing in the pitch-black trees.

    Slam against the piss-stained tiles:
      two girls coming home from a slumber party.

Silent in the corner as trains crash past,
our bodies' contorted clocks.

      A wing clamps shut the dark.

    o

      Hoktvlwv walks out in the moonrise.

She wakes the nightingales, pierces their throats,
steals the eggs and the blind chicks crackling.

The males are singing their joyous notes.

      Later I carried her into the woods—

scratched off sap—balm
for her body—stitched us

    a new bark throat.

    o

Tawny-feathered, sutured throat,
    night wind lashing the panes—

I wake up in damp sheets.

Old woman, immortal bird

run, mute, down the stairwell
dragging the little girl's shadow.

o

A shadow is a house made of hours.

She slips through the window
when the men are asleep
to sing, unseen
in moonlit boughs

her mute song buried in the valley.

o

I've seen the nightingale
rapping at the window,

heard her singing in pitch-black trees.

Buried beneath groceries on the plastic seat
of a crosstown train route's blinking streets

her old ghost, shuttling sloppy beside me,
nods, leers in dizzying lights.

Her eyes in the window are black,
wet. The milk I am carrying

burns in my lap.

○

She whistles to me from the valley—
a night wind whistling through birches.

Tethered by stirrups
to a wild horse, I am winged,
tearing through brambled clouds—

    awake in a bathtub to an old woman
    sponging down my bloody abrasions.

She braids my hair into a loose knot
as outside, apples
sink into the wet field.

○

I have grown a child of hours.

Sitting on a bench by the docked boats
Hoktvlwv approaches
with a shawl-covered cage,
    a plastic doll strapped to her breast.

I feed my crumbs to the birds
as they lurch, heads thrust
through grating—
        her gray teeth,
            sparked matches.

A little girl with cardboard wings
tugs at my dress. Barefoot

we shift down the littered street.

○

Hoktvlwv sleeps in her cardboard house.

In windows, birds
hang like wooden crosses,
wings ticktocking
the night's contorted face.

○

I have buried my song in the valley.

Left my hair,
knotted wreaths
for birds to comb from the ledge.

Old woman, immortal bird
perched in your silent, forever-green glade
will you weave me a nest,
lay me down in the shade?

I have slipped through the cracks
of the clock hands,
peeled the bark from my throat.

○

In gauze light—taut wings.

Net of blue veins,

slick black branches.

I gather a handful for the empty vase,
tell the girl:

> *leave the root in the ground,*
> *cut just above the node.*

> Harvesting songs from the valley,
> I lean into the scent of her tender skull—

her hair like the feathers
of this morning's nightingale
blown out on the roadside,

> bones scraping the sky.

WALLPAPER

Bright-spun
webs above the aquifer.

Humid streams, cottonmouths
cut through grass.

I clip the sheets
to last night's wind
then listen to its operatic shrill
through the tin roof—

ghosts of javelinas
gnashing at the screen door.

On telephone wires doves coo,
dip and swoop through soupy skies.

A dragonfly planes across the cornrows
where a cold snap killed the acanthus
pinking just days ago—

days late in their ceaseless bellow,
construction-paper animals
crossing the plains—

I trail them to the place
where flatness buckles,
steel tracks tilt the landscape,

where the wall splits—flame-tipped
painted aviary—

shredded yellow warbler,
beak stuffed with straw.

RIVER

If a sparrow were to sleep
in a depression in the ground
does it dream of the river
moving beneath it?

If a woman were to sleep
in the sparrow's breast.

A sparrow sleeps
in a depression in the ground.

If a woman were to curl
her body around it
she would no longer dream of the river.

They were walking in the reeds
along the riverbank. The river
they were moving toward
was moving backward.

She asked, what if we were to dream
each moment before us as we dream
each moment behind us?

They were walking in the reeds
along the riverbank. Said the deer,
it will feel like flying.

If the sparrow were to sleep
in the woman's breast.

If the woman were to lie
where the deer had lain, their dreams
depressions in the matted grass.

Watching the river, is she made of grass?

She is talking with the deer on the riverbank.
Or the sparrow, perched in the reeds.

She asks, as if time were a question.
She asks, will it feel like flying?

In a trench lined with asters,
new shoots of blue stem,
her dreams are the shape
of a question—her body
the dream of the river.

She says, it will feel like flying
watching the waves
pull against time.

She is made of time.

And she dreams of the deer
who shaped the trench—
watches the sparrow
fall from the sky.

PARADISE

We carried the swifts in wheelbarrow loads
from factory windows, chimneys.

Lit our fires with peat,
our backs to the murmuring forest.

After the rain, dust motes.
Ghosts in a glade of shade pine.

Now we no longer know the names
for flowers, cannot unfurl them
nor the stars' coils.

We flare in heaven's refinery,
raise our smoldering flag.

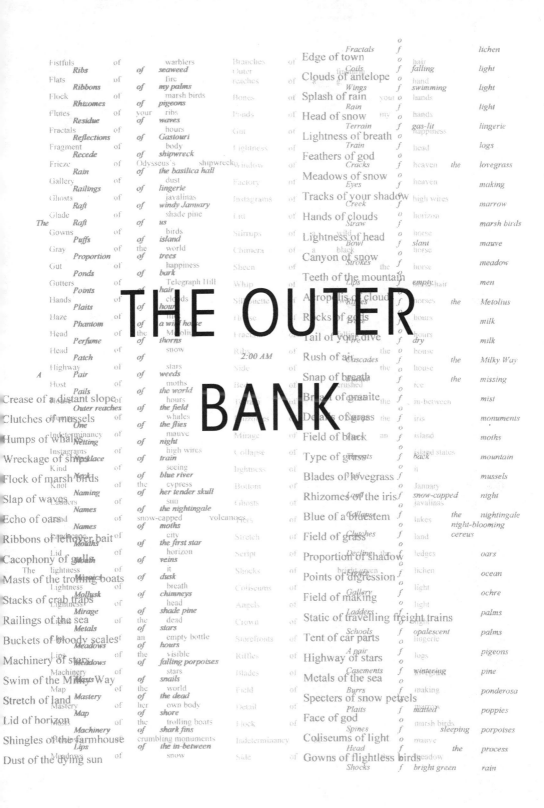

THE OUTER BANK

Fistfuls of
Ribs
Flats of
Ribbons of
Flock of
Rhizomes of
Flutes of
Residue your
Fractals of
Reflections of
Fragment of
Recede of
Frieze of
Rain
Gallery of
Railings
Ghosts of
Raft
Glade of
The *Raft* of
Gowns of
Puffs of
Gray of the
Proportion of
Gut of
Ponds
Gutters of
Points
Hands of
Plaits
Haze of
Phantom of
Head of the
Perfume the
Head of
Patch
Highway of
Pair
A
Host of
Pails of

Crease of a distant slope
Clutches of mussels
Humps of whales
Wreckage of ships
Flock of marsh birds
Slap of waves
Echo of oars
Ribbons of fender bait
Cacophony of gulls
Masts of the trolling boats
Stacks of crab traps
Railings of the sea
Buckets of bloody scales
Machinery of stars
Swim of the Milky Way
Stretch of land
Lid of horizon
Shingles of the farmhouse
Dust of the dying sun

warblers of
seaweed of
fire of
my palms
marsh birds of
pigeons
ribs your
waves of
hours of
Gastouri
body of
shipwreck
Odysseus's shipwreck
the basilica hall of
dust of
lingerie
javalinas of
windy Jamary
shade pine of
us
birds of
island of
world the
trees of
happiness of
bark
Telegraph Hill of
hair
clouds of
hours
a wind house of
the Metolius
thorns of
snow
stars of
weeds of
moths of
the world
hours of
the field of
whales of
the flies
mauve of
night
high wires of
train
seeing of
blue river
the cypress of
her tender skull
sun of
the nightingale
snow-capped volcanoes of
moths
city of
the first star
horizon of
veins
it of
dusk
breath of
chimneys
head of
shade pine
dead of
stars an
empty bottle of
hours
the visible of
falling porpoises
stars of
snails
world the
the dead of
own body her
shore of
trolling boats the
shark fins of
crumbling monuments
the in-between of
snow

Branches of
Outer
reaches of
Bones of
Ponds of
Gut of
Lightness of
window of
Factory of
Instagrams of
Lid of
Stirrups of
Chimera of
Sheen of
Whip of
Silhouettes of
Fractals of
Ribs of
2:00 AM of
Side of
Beads of
Brow of
Figures of
Mirage of
Collapse of
Lightness of
Bottom of
Ghosts of
Peers of
Stretch of
Script of
Shocks of
Coliseums of
Angels of
Crown of
Storefronts of
Rifles of
Blades of
Field of
Detail of
Flock of
Indeterminacy of
Side of

Fractals of
Edge of town o f
Coils o
Clouds of antelope f falling
fire swimming
Wings f
Splash of rain you o
Rain f
Head of snow my o
Terrain f gas-lit
Lightness of breath o
Train f head
Feathers of god o
Cracks f heaven the
Meadows of snow o
Eyes f heaven
Tracks of your shadow high wires
Creek o
Hands of clouds o horizon
Straw f
Lightness of head o horse
Bowl f slant
a black horse
Canyon of snow o
Strokes the o horse
Teeth of the mountain o
Lips f empty chair
Acropolis of clouds o
Rifles f horses the
Rocks of gods o
Bits f hours
Tail of your dive f hours
dry house
Rush of air the o
Cascades f house the
Snap of breath o
crushed f ice
Brow of granite f in-between
Depths of grass o
Figures the o iris
Field of black an f island
o
Type of grass o island states
back
Blades of lovegrass f
o
Rhizomes of the iris f January
snow-capped
Blue of a bluestem f javalinas
Collapse the
Field of grass f lakes land
Clutches o
Proportion of shadow ledges
Decline the o
birds green f lichen
Points of digression o
crushed f light
Gallery o
Field of making f light
Ladders o
Static of travelling freight trains f palms
Schools f opalescent
Tent of car parts f lingerie
A pair o
Highway of stars o logs
Casements f wintering
Metals of the sea o
Burrs f making
Specters of snow petrels o
Platts f matted
Face of god o
Spines f marsh birds sleeping
Coliseums of light o mauve
Head f the
Gowns of flightless birds meadow
Shocks f bright green

lichen
light
light
light
lingerie
logs
lovegrass
making
marrow
marsh birds
mauve
meadow
men
Metolius
milk
milk
Milky Way
missing
mist
monuments
moths
mountain
mussels
night
nightingale
night-blooming
cereus
oars
ocean
ochre
palms
palms
pigeons
pine
ponderosa
poppies
porpoises
process
rain

CATCH

Two hawks lash
    in the wind's net—
        listen to the distance
            they weave in the air
                between them
           your reflection
      pulls against currents. Fast
flash of clouds—
    first star's fin.

        Hawk-clawed my catch
              slips
       drowned in reeds—
         you swim
       wide-eyed
            suspended.

      Long cast
         a silver line
    threads the river's
           mouth shut.

        One hawk's
cry fades—dusk
          then rain.

     In the waning light
I reel in my line

    walk into the pines at the outer bank.

WINTER WATCH

—*Cannonball River, November 2016*

We commit ourselves to the count,
bees without a queen, swarming frozen ground.

Oatmeal, canned beans. Garlic salt, hominy.
White, brown, or wild rice.
                                    Rock salt. Flour.

The hours lift their lacy black veils—
a procession of women in mourning.

Startled, a doe slips into fog—a fugue
casts my shadow to the other side of grief,

leaves the body at the mudbank, gutted,
hoofprints trailing into winter wheat.

Lost, we talk of wilderness
and failure, time's sentient materialism,

the clock without hands now, without its tick—
awake snow-covered in a dead meadow

to sort more piles of things—no answer.
Fresh hay for horse feed, tipi poles, propane.

Hours like dull gold blow across the prairie
where Hoktvlwv travels to the inner reaches

alone, lantern clicking in the grass.
Brightness for a moment

until time returns—
how crowded this terminal of the world.

AFTERWEATHER

At a bend in the stream—
a clearing.

Ruby-crowned kinglets
trill from thickets.

    Green spears, lily-like
    clutch from a ditch.

First day of spring
gathering seeds—

       golden burrs of chinkapin

          buckthorn's blue-black berries—

            I stop to write
            and it snows in my notebook.

      ○

After snowfall
    willows
articulate themselves

slant toward the current
and freeze

sentenced above ice floes

to silence.

        ○

Build a small fire—

    dry sticks
          pinecone.

              Outside the window
                 the river is high

                 torrential under red-
                 stemmed dogwood.

        ○

The fire leapt
from ridge to ridge.   I carry your ashes through snow.

           Ice flakes
               blow over the river—

    cinders from the morning's stove.

        ○

Climb three tiers of lakes
          through towering tamaracks
lodgepole pine

      to scale the burn
          fossilized ice—

your steep trail heaped with obsidian.

                    o

Stitched across the eastern slope—

            saplings, green sprung.

                    Charcoal fingers
            claw the sky, roots—

                    a helix, dying spiders.

                    o

From a veiled ridge, mist
spills over the caldera.

            Throats of ponderosa
            crack in their icy casements.

                    Below me, Blue Lake
                    blinks its wide eye.

                    o

Blackened candles
        blistered bark
    owls
roosting in trees' charred snags—

                    no one to hear out here but wind—

    soot-stained chandeliers
            high in the old-growth pine—

white pine

Scotch pine

pitch pine—

bleached burnt-out mansion.

o

After the settling of scoria and ash
clear water fills the basin.

I wash in the deep
glaciated canyon—

    smoke-blue water
    flecked with green—

        half-drowned logs
        scarved with moss.

o

Lichens
    bright lime
cling to damp bark.

    Fallen trees
wedged into banks
    make pools for Chinook
redband trout.

Where the earth is soft
        skeletons of elk
surface clean from snowmelt.

                    ○

Winter's lake
        vanished
into a meadow.

Wild asparagus
        wood leeks
shoot up from muddy seeps.

I balance on spines
of sunken giants—

        plaited waves
                matted grass—

        if I could bury you
                        here, at last.

                    ○

Days when there is sun
I carry a book
to the clearing at the stream's bend.

            The wind
                spring friend
                    picks its dark pages.

APRICOTS

A light.
A room.
Lakes upon lakes.

The hen's head, blazing
drops to the mat.

I want to sleep in the straw
through the slant afternoon,
my own head a bowl of apricots.

Were the blood tracks
on the forested overpass
not the antelope's.

Were the thunder
clouds in my belly
not the dark strokes of men.

There is no man in a tower
with a stopwatch.

Tonight no moon
to break myself against.

A light.
A boat.
Unlit room.

Don't sleep yet.
I'm rowing toward you.

LOST COAST

The continent is dismantling.

I go to its shores—
the outer reaches of a fracturing hand.

I go to its shores to feed the black swans.

○

She birthed twin girls
by blowing sand
from her palm's crease—

moon unsheathed from clouds,

cities bloomed from her mouth.

○

The city is a ship in a bottle.

Streets glitter, crack.

An old man pushes a walker up the gutters of Telegraph Hill.

Dense fog spills over studded chimneys, flickering rooms, women
smoking cigarettes behind wedding shrouds.

A banker throws himself in front of a commuter train during rush hour
traffic.

Hoktvlwv in a yellow raincoat scans high wires for her shoes.

It is Tuesday, I tow my trash to the curb—

all is tilted toward the sea.

o

I dig myself a bed
for flowers, plant
in each eye
gardenias.

Turn away
from the mirror
to call your lost name—

a white moon folds
my black photograph.

o

She folds a swan
from the black photograph.

Opens her palms—

blows birds like dry leaves
toward the pond

where two women drift by
in a raft of reeds, green

ribbons braiding shut

their blue mouths.

o

Hoktvlwv plucks a gardenia.

Afloat in a liquid world
she was seasick with the restless
wingbeat of birds, circling the moon
she carried inside her.

Her body split into continents.

Her breath became the name of all things.

o

Often I have gone to the sea
and not been able to find it.

o

The city with her rudders and sails
sluices north,
trawling for light.

The sea turns in her lapis gown,
the sky a flowered
shawl she tosses.

I weave the clouds from birds
passing over: yesterday
black birds. Today, blue.

This continent is a memory

remapped each morning—

seashells washed upon the beach,
each breath a naming of you.

o

My body is a drowning city.

I crush an old cigarette butt into the dust.

The southeastern deltas
will soon be blooming. Soon
the ark will sail on without me.

I unlatch my suitcase—
blue dresses spill out.

On the plastic raft
I clutch my trash.

Black swans gather on shore.

o

It isn't possible to disappear
from that which has disappeared.

If I were to touch the sea
I may not breathe again.

Not the same
breath. Not
the same hands.

Disassembled by the sea
the city collects itself
ravenously around me.

On the avenues, starlings
sweep through the flutes of my ribs.

o

In the twilight gray
of the visible world

where the shore is ambiguous
and clams rock shut

I gather eelgrass
tangled in foam

weave a raft of seaweed
beneath the churning fog

blow white sand
from the creases of my palm

until there is only
one woman in the sea

and me in the remains
of a coastal city

unclipping blue dresses
from the wind.

o

Dawn light rustles
the hillside's weeds, night's trash
trapped in trees.

Awake to the pigeon's
relentless thrum, slow
rapture, drum wave—

    you are the song that recedes.

I arrange blue stones
around the boundary of my feet,

fold the photographs
into two black swans,

drop them among the gardenias
and reeds where a woman
lays flattened,
her blue beak open.

        ∘

On the treadmill by the window on the corner of 16th and De Haro,
I name the pigeons, high wires, green car, blue. There must be other
names for metal boxes, electrical labyrinths rigged across the sky. Other
names for blue. Other than sea. Not all birds that live in the city are
pigeons. Not all are birds. I strap myself into the rowing machine. What
an exile. What dry land, wet air, flowers breaking through windows.

        ∘

It is Tuesday. Alone on a bench
at the edge of the continent
I watch the streets of heaped glass

sift and shimmer under fast
black clouds as the city
snags back her blue
memory with her teeth.

Loneliness is an element
like water or wind.
There is no sea here.
Only what is still
has memory.
In the pond
two black swans
sail through my reflection.

DESCENT

I have drunk the night's perfumes

      poured tea:
            batched leaves of the sea's decay

    tumbleweed

  chokecherry

    skeleton leaf

To ascend, I read
    you must first descend—go out

      a different way
    than the way you came in

Dawn comes, a lambent orb

      hovers above the plains—a woman
         robed in red-stitched silk

  flames at the railroad trestle

          Spanish dagger

  flat-lined horizon

      black angus grazing in creosote

Wind whips dust

into a slender column

pirouetting over parched fields

no song for the snakes
in the dun-colored grass

no doves
no Lucifer hummingbirds

Clouds, noctilucent

portend tornadoes—antelope
cram into gabled

chambers—I rattle through pink
ocotillos

siphon the sand
from my throat

At the crack in the road
where sky bleeds through

I wrap myself
in thunder's
rolling cloak
and dive

HOKTVLWV'S CROW

There were still songbirds then
nesting in hackberry trees
and a butterfly named *Question*.

I remember ivy trembling
at the vanishing point of your throat.

Then the timelines crashed.
California split into an archipelago.
Orchards withered under blooms of ash.

Now there is no nectar. No rotten fruit.
The air is quiet.

                Once, in Russia,
Ornithologists trapped
a population of hooded crows,
transported them 500 miles
westward. Winter came.
They never caught up with their flock.

With crusts of calcified algae
we catalogue each day lost:
hot thermals, cirrus vaults,
fistfuls of warblers hurtling into dark.

There was no sound to the forgetting.
We knew the heart would implode
before the breath and lungs collapsed.

That the world would end in snow,
an old woman walking alone,
empty birdcage strapped to her back.

ABOUT THE AUTHOR

Jennifer Elise Foerster is an alumna of the Institute of American Indian Arts, received her MFA in writing from the Vermont College of Fine Arts, and is a PhD candidate in English and Creative Writing at the University of Denver. Foerster is the recipient of a 2017 NEA Creative Writing Fellowship, a Lannan Foundation Writing Residency Fellowship, and was a Wallace Stegner Fellow in Poetry at Stanford University. A member of the Muscogee (Creek) Nation of Oklahoma, Foerster is the author of one previous book of poems, *Leaving Tulsa* (University of Arizona Press 2013).